W9-BXY-149

October 5, 2004

Dear Chris:

Congratulations on successfully completing the MIT program! I'm sure you're very excited and looking forward to assuming your new responsibilities.

Twenty three years ago I was at the very same stage in my career – recently completing the MIT program, loaded with excitement and great intentions, but deep down lacking some confidence about whether I had what it takes to be successful. Over the years, I learned many lessons the hard way. But I quickly found that the amount of initiative I displayed related directly to my career growth. I strongly suggest you take full advantage of the knowledge of key teammates, other managers, your General Manager, and your Director.

Which brings me to the reason for this letter. Between my office and home I recently counted 147 different management/leadership books that I have bought for myself, been given, or acquired by attending some type of training program or seminar. To be perfectly honest, I have completely read only a small percentage of these books. Most contained a few good points, but eventually became bogged down in theory, mumbo-jumbo, complex strategies, and complicated formulas. I would quickly become bored, and the book would go on the shelf to collect dust.

Because of my past experiences, I was delighted when I discovered the enclosed book – ABCs of

THE

ABC's

OF HOSPITALITY MANAGEMENT

BY HOWARD CUTSON, FMP

FORWARD BY STEPHEN MICHAELIDES

CST PUBLICATIONS, HUDSON, OHIO

Photo Credit:

Author's Photo: Sharon A. Pecoraro, Hudson, Ohio

Library of Congress Catalog Card Number:

98-093508

ISBN 0-9666582-0-5

First Printing: August 1998
Printed and Bound in the United States of America

CST Publications (800) 776-7988
FAX: (330) 656-3335

THIS BOOK IS DEDICATED TO
LORAINE, PATRICIA, AND SHARON...
THE LADIES OF MY LIFE, WHO'VE
TRIED TO KEEP ME ON THE
STRAIGHT AND NARROW.

TABLE OF CONTENTS

FORWARD...

A few things up front...a disclaimer of sorts: Howard Cutson paid me a few bucks to help him edit this gem of a book. But, if my fingerprints are on it, they are so faint that not even the most competent cop could lift them from it's pages. *The ABC's of Hospitality Management* is Howard's voice and what a crystal clear and lucid voice it is.

There are dozens of these kinds of books out there. I know. I've read or skimmed through most of them. What's most remarkable about Howard's book is its clarity. You will find no equivocation here, no mumbo-jumbo, and no formulaic strategies that render so many management texts impossible to understand.

This is straightforward advice devoid of theoretical jargon and presumptions.

This is instruction based on the countless hours Howard has spent in the hospitality trenches. What he proves here is that you can work in this marvelous business and learn – as he has learned – to love and respect it; to realize that only a few careers compare to the rewards and pleasures you can derive from working in the hospitality industry.

So, what's Howard's book about? Well, it's about surviving, coping, strategizing, learning, dealing, working, and hoping. Ultimately, it's about running your business – about being productive, efficient, and making a buck or two. It's about relationships: the communion you establish with your employees and superiors; with your customers and suppliers. It's about doing all of this and more, just so, at the end of the day, week, month, or year, you can look back and say to yourself that you put forth your best effort. You can be delighted that you have energized yourself and your employees to develop a culture that produces results everyone is proud to be part of.

Is this book for you? You bet it is.

First and foremost, it's for the person who has just been asked to manage. That's what Howard says in his introduction. Howard is only partly right.

This book is for everyone. In addition to the brand new manager fishing about for advice, suggestions, and ideas on ways to manage well, it's also for the entry-level employee anxious to learn what this business is all about; it's for the community college grad who has set his sights on a career in hospitality... but isn't quite sure what's demanded, expected, or required of him. It's for the human resource person of a restaurant or hotel chain to distribute to unit managers or to those who aspire to that slot; it's for HRI and culinary school instructors to share with their students. It's for editors of the business press so that when they write about the hospitality industry, they have a better, deeper appreciation of what it takes to work in it. Finally, it's for the seasoned manager or executive – perhaps the president of a chain, the owner/chef of a restaurant, the hotel executive – who wants to review the basics, just so she can recall what the orientation and drills were like; just so she can be a bit more understanding and compassionate of those who come to work for her, who might not be as accomplished as their resumes make them out to be.

There is no plot progression to Howard's book. *The ABC's of Hospitality Management* is not a novel. As he says in his introduction, "you don't have to read everything at one sitting...but do eventually read everything." You can, if you like, read it from cover to cover – from first page to last, as it were – or you can pick it up and turn to any page or any chapter. Whatever your routine, wherever you stop, you will know that you've learned something of value that you can put to use immediately.

Stephen Michaelides

Stephen Michaelides is President of Words, Ink., a Cleveland-based business-to-business communications company. Before that, he was, for 27 years, editor and associate publisher of Restaurant Hospitality *magazine.*

INTRODUCTION...

To those of you who are new to this industry called, "Hospitality," a warm welcome. To those of you who have been around for a while, but are now just entering the management arena, get set for some new insights and perspectives that you probably never experienced or, perhaps, never knew existed.

You'll find here a collection of brief essays on a number of management topics often overlooked in school or in your company's management training programs.

In over 30 years of studying the hospitality industry – from a wide variety of viewpoints – I've seen many a new manager struggle or, worse, fail totally, unable to cope with the intensity and pressures of this business because he or she wasn't trained effectively or appropriately.

Let's assume that you've joined your company as a manager fresh out of hotel school, or you have just been promoted "out of the ranks." Too often, here is what you're told: "You just graduated from that big hotel school. Show me your stuff. Use what they taught you."
Or, "You've been one of our best employees.

Your new job will come naturally. Don't
worry about it." Sound familiar?

Result? You stumble – in front of employees
and guests. That doesn't surprise me.
Studies show that managers in foodservice
confront 50 to 100 percent more decisions
daily than managers in any other industry.
Some welcome, huh?

The flip side is that this can be one of the
most rewarding and enjoyable businesses to
be a part of. It can provide instant
gratification within an environment and
culture that is ever changing. It's loaded with
wonderful people... other managers,
employees, and yes, even customers.

It's hard work, long hours, and lots of
frustration. Any job worth hanging onto is
saddled with those conditions. How you cope
is what this book is all about. It'll help soften
some of those frustrations, make those long
hours tolerable, even enjoyable.

The essays are short and to the point. Each
topic stands on it's own. Pick a topic that
interests you. Start anywhere you'd like. You
don't have to read everything at one sitting.
However, do eventually read everything,
thinking, as you read, how each topic applies
to and influences your work.

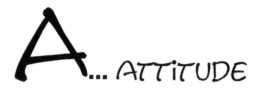

A... ATTITUDE

"It's usually attitude, not aptitude that takes you to the top of your profession." So says world-renowned super-salesman and motivational speaker Zig Ziglar.

In a business as people-intensive as ours, the ability to please customers, motivate employees to do the same, and stay focused on personal goals, is totally based on personal attitude.

As a manager, you set the attitude for your entire operation. There's an old saying, "The fish smells from the head first" As the head fish, if you are having a bad day, guess what...your entire team will have one. If you are excited and motivated – guess what? So is your entire team. Your team suddenly hit the "zone" and can handle more than they ever thought possible - and much better than you ever thought possible!

Get out on the wrong side of the bed and no one does anything right. The bottom line? Your attitude carries a tremendous amount of weight and influence. You have an impact on guest satisfaction and employee performance every time you walk into your operation.

I even know of operations where the team watches out the window when the manager drives up to see whether he slams the car door or not. They instantly know what kind of day they are going to have!

If you want your people to smile, you have to greet them with a warm, sincere smile every day. Don't ever think that a paycheck is a substitute for a genuine, heartfelt smile, warm greeting and sincere "Thank you."

If you want a super sales team, you've got to be a super salesperson yourself. Don't just set the target, be the exemplary role model when it comes to guest interaction.

If you want change to happen, you must believe in the change and convince others, by your tone of voice and continued reinforcement, that the change is worthwhile. Remember, monotony (the absence of change) stifles momentum.

If you want your guests leaving your operation raving about food and service, you must establish a personal attitude of excellence and train your employees to deliver at that level. Once you and your team reach that level of excellence, raise the bar! Move to that next higher level of excellence. Let up just one day, and you run the risk of losing momentum...and return guests.

Change and excellence go hand in hand.

Before leaving the topic of attitude, here's a word of caution. It is rare to find the attitudes of your employees totally in synch with yours. Your job is to move them close to your goals and expectations. Your attitude, your exemplary behavior (no task is too easy or too hard for you; no task is beneath you), your willingness to listen to ideas that effect change set the mood for reaching those goals. No one said it was easy!

We all do have one thing in common. No matter where we live, who we work for, what our job, who we have as friends, **we all listen to one radio station - *WII-FM.*** It's the universal station, the great determiner of attitude, the mood manager, the productivity producer, the prophet of profit.

WII-FM. The call letters stand for **"What's In It For Me?"** Once you honestly answer that question for yourself and for each of your employees and customers, you're on your way "to the top" together! Once you establish what the benefits are, the behaviors that attain them transform the attitudes as well. Capture their interest and you hold attitudes in the palm of your hand. And...don't forget, that applies to you, too!

A... ABSENTEEISM

Absenteeism and tardiness are your first indications of a morale problem. Both are extremely contagious, sometimes even leading to catastrophe. It doesn't matter whether it is one employee or the entire crew.

When mediocre employees see their peers enjoying frequent tardiness or call-ins without response or repercussion, they wonder whether they can get away with the same infractions.

However, when your *best employees* see people getting away with being late or calling off, they *leave* you and search for another job where they don't have to carry more than their share of the load.

That's a catastrophe! Especially when you consider how difficult it is to find quality employees these days.

Make sure your absenteeism and tardiness policies are clear *and in writing.* Review them thoroughly before hiring someone. Review them again at orientation. Give each new employee a copy of the policy and post one at the time clock.

Most critical - administer your policy fairly and evenly. No pet employees... No scapegoats... No selective memory.

R... BUDGET

If you don't know where you are going, it doesn't matter train, plane, bus, or cab you get into. If you don't have a target, it doesn't matter where or how you shoot the arrow. As trite as they sound, these old saws represent an important concept in business: *If you want to move your business, the first step is to determine where you want to take it.*

Budgeting is a necessary evil that is often terribly overdone by corporations and totally ignored by the independent operators among us. The best policy seems to lie somewhere in-between.

If you want to be successful in the hospitality business, you must have an excellent grasp of the numbers needed to achieve that simple little 6-letter goal - **PROFIT.**

Then, and only then, can you develop the action plans necessary to get you there.

When you don't take the time to develop a plan, a budget, a set of goals, you often find yourself making lots and lots of false starts - activities which take you in a myriad of directions and confuse the heck out of your employees, your customers, and even yourself. When nobody knows what you are or where you are going, one thing is for sure - your business is in trouble.

Creating an effective budget gives you the basis for the development of employee and management goals, marketing efforts, menu refinements, service training, hours of operation, and much more. It keeps you and your employees focused on current conditions that drive the business and how those conditions will influence the future of the business. It keeps you from dwelling on the past.

Budgets are only effective when actual results are frequently and accurately compared to your budgeted projections. You may think your projections are realistic, but when your results don't match, your projections are just wishful thinking.

Don't wait too long to analyze those projections and results. Budgets should be broken into sensible and workable accounting periods, ones which are long enough to collect meaningful data, but short enough to give you speedy response times when you find a problem. Most of us find a monthly or 4-week period to be just about right.

If we go much beyond that period in evaluating our past performance versus budget, we lose the ability to quickly regain control of problematic areas, thereby running the risk of losing significant profit dollars.

Once you've run your monthly profit and loss statement, compare it to:

➡ your projection for that month

➡ results from the last operating month

➡ results for the same month last year

Look at and make note of:

➡ real numbers

➡ developing trends

➡ unusual factors which might have impacted on your business that month,

➡ your budget for the next accounting period.

Analyze trends to determine their staying power; analyze unusual (i.e., unpredictable) factors to determine what chances they have of recurring. Then establish the action plans, which will help put you on that budget by the end of the following month.

If you are like me, you don't like surprises. The best way to avoid them is to develop and use a workable budget. Don't write it and bury it in a drawer until the end of the quarter or the end of the year. Use it as an intimate business advisor - one that can help you take your business where you want to go with it.

Before we leave the topic of budgeting, we should spend a few minutes addressing the kinds of information you need to include in a budget.

The key with budgets, just like any other aspect of your business, is to break the information into small, meaningful pieces. Make the pieces small enough to help you identify specific areas, which need to be controlled and monitored separately, but large enough that you are not spending needless hours dissecting meaningless individual accounts.

For example, today if you run a bar, it is essential that you track your spirit, imported beer, American beer, wine by the bottle, wine by the glass, and non-alcohol beverages separately. If you don't break the categories down at least this far; you can't determine where the cost problem lies. Maybe a perceived a cost problem is merely a change in sales trends.

On the other hand, in a restaurant, you may not need to break down your meat cost categories into levels smaller than beef-pork-veal-lamb-etc., unless you are having significant problems controlling one of those costs.

Don't forget to involve your entire team in the budgeting process. It gives them greater ownership in their efforts to achieve those budgets.

Be sure to share your operating results with your team as well. Let them know every month how the operation compared to budget. Recognize their achievements when they are good – when they help you meet or exceed projections; and, when they don't – yes, it does occasionally happen - help them develop the plans to improve on poor performance.

When you don't share this information with your team, they can't effectively help you manage your budget and grow your business.

Besides, we've found that when you don't share your operating results with your team, they OVERESTIMATE how well you are doing... often by up to **400 percent**; and that can lead to significant problems such as waste or even theft.

One final thought. If your performance consistently falls short of your budget, don't automatically blame your team. It may be that your budget is unrealistic.

C...COMPLAINT HANDLING

No one ever takes the time to teach new managers how to properly handle complaints, yet it is often one of the first things they're faced with. And it sure can be intimidating. Right?

Here's some sound advice:

✓   Get to the guest ASAP.

✓   Come down to their level. Don't tower over them. Your intent is to listen to the complaint and, then, resolve it. Body language and your physical relationship with the customer sends a message about how serious and sincere you are.

✓   Stay calm and professional.

✓   Apologize - often that's all a customer wants.

✓ Remove the cause of the problem at once.

✓ Ask how the guest would like the situation resolved. They often want less than you'd think. Be sure the question takes the form of a polite request, not a challenge. Remember that coming up with a solution is still your responsibility, not the guest's.

✓ Don't argue. You can never win an argument with a guest.

✓ Take immediate action.

✓ Exceed their expectations - do more than you have to.

✓ Thank them for helping you improve.

✓ Once you've resolved the complaint, make sure you find the root cause of the complaint and correct it.

✓ Follow up, either with a phone call or note.

C... CUSTOMER

When giving workshops around the country, I will often ask the group to list their greatest assets. The typical answers are, "our employees," "our chef," "our unique menu," "the one-of-a-kind atmosphere." All good answers. But, what is your true number one asset?

YOUR GUESTS! YOUR CUSTOMERS!

That wasn't so hard, was it?

Your customers are literally your "reason for being." Without your customers, you can have the greatest chef, the most provocative ambiance in the world, but...need I go on?

Your guests' needs come before all others; before your needs, before your employees', before your boss's.

Your customers pay your wages. They pay your food and labor costs, your fixed costs.

They help you employ a lot of people. They even help you pay your taxes – all of them. And guess what, if you have expansion plans, who do you think supplies some of that money for expansion?

It's your job, as a manager, to help create and continue to mold and refine your product - your overall operation from front to back - that keeps them your customers coming back again and again.

There is nothing better, in business, than a solid, growing base of *regular* customers.

Stu Leonard, one of the most interesting food retailers in contemporary history, has chiseled his customer policy into a large rock just outside the front door of his store:

"Rule #1: The customer is always right.

Rule #2: If the customer is ever wrong, reread Rule #1."

OK. Maybe Mr. Leonard's policy isn't 100 per cent on target. I'm sure we can both come up with many examples of notable exceptions. However, if you take that policy and modify it slightly, you will end up with the most important credo we can ever establish to assure our future success:

Rule #1: The customer likes to be right.

Rule #2: If the customer is ever wrong, never tell them.

Rule #3: Never let them leave without making what's wrong, right.

Customers buy when they feel good about themselves and what they are buying. Telling customers they are wrong about something convinces them to go somewhere else - where they can feel "right."

Bottom line? It's a lot cheaper to buy a dinner for an irate guest than to assume you'll find a replacement just by running that expensive display ad in the newspaper. Better yet, it's even less expensive to spend money upfront with proper training and high-quality product to assure that all of your guests leave your place content and thinking about the next time they plan to visit.

Make them feel wanted. Make them feel important. Make them feel special. Most importantly, make them want to come back again and again. Work your dining room. Find out what your customers like and don't like. Listen to them carefully. They offer invaluable advice that you can not get from anyone else. I've learned, (often the hard way) and you will too, that what they have to say is often a good indicator of what is really going on in your place.

Remember this... if you hear a complaint from only one guest out of a hundred, you have a major problem! Surveys have found that only three or four guests out of every 100 guests ever bother to complain. The other 97 just make a point of telling from eight to 20 of their friends, who then tell 3-4 of their friends, and so on and so on. Pretty soon, no one wants to patronize your place, based on hearsay evidence from a handful of people, *some of whom never set foot in your place.*

The Small Business Administration advises that 68 per cent of customers who leave you, do so because of an attitude of indifference on the part of an employee. Can you afford those warm bodies and not hire the best people you can find and train them better than anyone else?

Customers are your only bankable assets. How you invest in them will determine how your investment grows.

D...DELEGATION

You're a manager. One person. You can't do everything yourself. Management is defined as getting things done through others. If you are always doing, you can't be managing. It's impossible.

If you schedule yourself to cover an employee station, no one is effectively managing the overall operation. You have become one of your employees in a manager-less operation. The money you think you save by doing an employee's job is lost ten-fold when you neglect the big picture.

The key to effective delegation lies in hiring the best people, developing them through outstanding training, and then empowering them to do what they were hired to do without having to depend on you for every decision.

$\mathcal{D}$...DEVELOPMENT

It's growing yourself and your people. It's training. It's teaching competencies.

As a manager, you are responsible for the development of your own skills and those of your employees. When you effectively use your human resources, you're getting the most out of your physical resources as well; and that, ultimately, benefits your customers and your company. It also improves interactivity among employees and results in their working efficiently and compatibly as a team.

If you and your team are not always moving forward, improving every day, building on your momentum, learning something new whenever possible, stagnation and complacency take over.

Try to remember these key concepts when developing people:

❶ Not every one learns new skills at the same rate. Some people are quick studies and pick up new skills and concepts the first time you show them. Others take much longer - almost to the point of frustration - but, once they catch on, they may actually be better than any one else at that new skill. It can be *very frustrating;* just don't give up on them too soon.

Speaking of repetition, did you know that studies have shown most people don't even hear a message until it has been repeated six times? It takes 15 repetitions for the message to sink in. It takes 21 or more reinforcements to break an old habit, start a new one, or establish a new behavior pattern.

So, don't expect your employees to be "trained" after one lecture or demonstration. Ever try to go on a diet or stop smoking? Can't do it in one day, can you?

❷ The second key to development is that everyone learns differently. Some people are visual learners. They learn by reading instructions or watching a demonstration. Some people are auditory learners. They learn best by listening. And some people are kinesthetic learners. They learn best by doing. Practice. Role-play. The truth is that we all learn best by involving all three methods and as many senses as possible.

Keep in mind that sales and service skills (front desk, Host, server, management, et al) can be learned *only by doing.* You've got to involve the employee in lots and lots of role-play. For most of us, sales skills and interacting with customers are outside our comfort zones. We need plenty of time and practice before we work with real, live customers.

❸   Another key point to remember is that most people have very short attention spans in a training environment. I've heard some experts estimate it to be as short as *40 seconds!*

❹   The best way to develop and train your people? Daily 5-10 minute training sessions involving visual, auditory, and interactive role-play activities.

No, I didn't forget about your development.

①   Go to every seminar and workshop you can.

②   Listen to every training and motivational tape you can get your hands on.

③   Visit your competitors. When you travel, find out the names of successful operations in the cities you're in and visit them; talk to the owners.

④   Read the business press. They are full of great ideas that can enhance your development.

⑤   Ask questions of your boss...and your employees.

⑥   Try things you've never tried before.

⑦   Talk and listen to everyone you meet.

⑧   Think in terms of "what if?"

⑨   Open your mind and discover the world around you as if you were a two-year-old again. You'll learn more than you ever thought possible.

⑩   Think like a customer

E... EMPLOYEES

Here's a revelation on a major component of success: You must treat your employees exactly the same way as you treat your most important guests.

How do you attract, develop, and keep, the best employees? Doesn't matter with whom you are dealing - X-Generation or the seasoned pro - the guidelines are pretty much the same.

When you think about it, they're the same guidelines, which keep you happy and motivated at your job.

The keys? Here we go...

TREAT THEM LIKE INDIVIDUALS.

Why? Because that's what they are. Not everyone will have the same goals or work ethic. Not everyone is looking for the same career path you are on. Not everyone is working just for the money (although they all want some). Not everyone longs for overtime.

How do you know who wants what or what motivates whom? It's so easy, it's scary! TALK TO THEM! Ask questions about their hobbies and their families. Find out what turns them on and what turns them off. In a very real sense, you will be expanding upon those issues and concerns you discussed superficially when you were interviewing. You will learn how to motivate them and, at the same time, you will make them feel important.

And please, don't forget...know their names and use them often. There is no greater stroke than using someone's name - especially when it's combined with a "Thank You." On the flip side, I'll bet you can still remember the time someone referred to you as "hey, you," or "tiger." Not very pleasant, was it?

CREATE A TEAM ATMOSPHERE

Your employees want to feel that they are part of a team. The Twentysomething Generation often responds very positively to a family-like involvement, which many didn't get at home!

Proper use of TLC works wonders, but remember, IT MUST BE SINCERE. Most employees can spot a phony a mile away. Once you've been pegged as one, you've lost a most important leverage - respect and the ability to be taken seriously.

Now, I'm not asking you to "baby" your employees. Just treat with them with respect; help them as they help you reach your goals by helping them reach theirs as well.

GET THEM INVOLVED

The best way I've found to achieve goals is to let your employees help you establish those goals. (see **Goals)** Ownership works wonders. Who knows the most about what is going on in your business? That is, besides your customers? Your employees. Ask questions and *listen carefully* to the answers you get. Most of them will make tremendous sense. Rhetorical questions are the tools of blowhards; they ask them just to hear themselves talk. They are not looking for answers; they're just out to prove how smart they are. Don't use them!

The key? Do something with the input you get. Otherwise you quickly lose credibility and loyalty.

Be sure you give them plenty of notice when it comes to change. More importantly, when you tell them about change, make sure it happens. While we may be uncomfortable with change, the biggest discomfort comes when promised changes never happen.

Be sure to share company information with them. Sales and profits will improve faster if everyone is pulling in the same direction with a full understanding of how far you have to go.

GIVE THEM WELL-DEFINED STANDARDS OF PERFORMANCE

Write them out. Be specific Repeat: be specific. Be realistic. Repeat: be realistic. Nothing turns off an employee more than ambiguous standards and standards impossible to fulfill.

Train your employees how to deliver your standards. Remember that many young people have not been exposed to the standards of hospitality we're accustomed to. They are fully capable of meeting them, they just sometimes need help understanding them and understanding why they are important. Don't forget, for a lot of young people, restaurant service has consisted of a fast food take-out window.

So, when you are training, tell them not only your standards, but also how and why they must be met.

GIVE FEEDBACK OFTEN

Your employees want to know how they are doing. They want to feel they are making progress, especially if they are considering a career in foodservice. It's your job to tell them where they stand. Praising is positive reinforcement. Use it often to recognize and reward improvement or special effort. DO IT IN FRONT OF OTHERS WHENEVER POSSIBLE! It's great for morale; it may motivate others to strive for the same recognition. It's called creating an atmosphere of healthy competition. Remember though, praise must be sincere and relate to real performance.

At the same time, you want to look out for less than acceptable performance. When you spot it, address it immediately. When you are inconsistent in maintaining standards or when you treat some employees differently from others, it's noticed immediately. And there goes morale. You want dissension among the ranks? Manipulate standards to accommodate the eccentricities of a favored employee.

EXPECT AND INSPECT DAILY

Remember, you're a manager, not a mother.

Handle reprimands, negative feedback and criticism in private at all times. Always criticize the action not the person. Think back on what we discussed earlier about the number of times something has to be repeated before it takes hold. Remedial training might be in order!

The Golden Rule used to be quoted as:

Treat others the way you want them to treat you.

Today's Golden Rule:

Treat others the way they would like you to treat them.

Most of the time, it ends up the same way you want to be treated anyway!

E...EXIT INTERVIEW

If you are about to lose one of your better employees, you want to find out why he or she is leaving.

Ask the hard questions, insist on candor, and listen to the answers, even if you don't want to hear them. You can't afford to lose more valued employees because of problems or misperceptions you could correct if you knew about them.

Who knows, you might even save the employee. Maybe all that is needed is a small adjustment in the workload or schedule. Maybe all she wanted was to vent. If you can't salvage the situation, make sure she knows that she is welcome to return.

Often, greener pastures turn out to be short-lived or even an illusion, but embarrassment keeps proud employees from admitting a mistake and returning. Don't let that happen. Good employees are just too hard to find.

Finally, here's a caution. In the course of the exit interview, you may find out that you are part of the problem. Acknowledge and confront it. Deal with it.

F ...FEEDBACK

Feedback...better known as *The Breakfast of Champions.* You just can't get enough! Every day, every meal, everywhere in your operation, talk to your employees and customers. Professor Michael LeBoeuf would tell you to ask them two very important questions:

How are we doing?

How can we make your experience better?

And, do I have to repeat myself? Listen to what they have to say!

F ...FiVE SENSES

Most people have five senses: sight, smell, taste, hearing, and touch. A few folks are missing one, or even two. Some claim to have a sixth, or even a seventh. No matter how many, one thing is for sure. Your customers evaluate your operation with all of their senses.

To be an effective manager, learn to do the same. It's the only way you can truly understand how your customers rate you.

SIGHT:

⇒ Are all the lights on that should be on?

⇒ Do all areas look clean - inside and out?

⇒ Does your place look organized and ready for business?

⇒ How about your employees? Clean, organized, alert, ready for business?

⇒ Does your operation look guest-friendly and inviting?

SMELL:

⇒ What odors **or** aromas meet your guests when they arrive - inside and out?

⇒ Any smells around the trash area?

⇒ What do the rest rooms smell like?

⇒ Do your foods and beverages smell fresh and appetizing?

⇒ Do your people smell fresh and clean? No heavy colognes or perfumes?

TASTE:

⇒ Do your foods and beverages taste wholesome, fresh, and authentic?

⇒ Do flavor combinations blend well; are they compatible?

⇒ Are there any outstanding, distinctive flavors that guests can get only at your place? Are they better than they can get anywhere else?

HEARING:

⇒ Is there pleasant music playing in the background? Or is there offensive, loud noise from the kitchen or dishwasher?

⇒ Do you hear employees interacting cordially with guests?

⇒ Do you hear the sounds of sizzling food or brewing cappuccino? Do you hear the sounds of glasses clinking?

⇒ Are guests chatting comfortably or whispering quietly? Does the volume of noise in your operation overpower conversation, making it difficult to talk?

⇒ What are guests talking about? If it's your place, is it positive?

TOUCH:

⇒ Are all guest-contact surfaces clean and well maintained?

⇒ Is your furniture comfortable and inviting?

⇒ Is temperature pleasant and comfortable?

Tomorrow, walk through your operation and "five-sense" it. Just like your guests will do. Do it several times a day... and don't forget to correct or improve the areas that need it.

Ps: We'll be happy to send you a free copy of our Five Senses Checklist© Just send a self-addressed, stamped envelope to: Cutson Associates, 589 Atterbury Blvd., Hudson 44236.

**If you are not
having fun...
get out of this
business.**

**It's too challenging
an industry to play
it any other way.**

G...GOALS

Goals, like standards, are meaningless unless you write them down. If they exist only in our heads, they tend to get lost or totally forgotten amidst the clutter of everyday distractions. Once they're on paper, they seem to haunt us until we have attained them.

Who needs goals?

Everyone in your operation...from top to bottom.

Who should write these goals?

The people who have to attain them - with a little help from you, of course. Just to make sure their goals are in sync with the overall goals of the operation. More on this later.

How many goals do your people need?

Only three or four at any given time. More than that and goals lose their impact, their power, their influence. Too many goals intimidate with the sheer weight of their number. Result? Too many excuses for not attaining them. Besides, there's nothing wrong with adding new goals as existing ones are met. Just be fair about it.

Be sure to make a couple of the goals short-term and a couple long-term. Sure feels great to get some out of the way soon, doesn't it?

What makes a good goal?

Good goals are *SMART* goals...*S*pecific, *M*easurable, *A*ction-oriented, *R*ealistic, and *T*ime-bound. If a goal does not have *all* of these qualities, it is not a goal.

Don't forget, today employees always want to know *why.* You must be prepared to explain their goals; tell them *why* they need to attain them, *why* change is necessary, *why* their efforts are important to the success of the operation.

Share the background information with them. If it's a goal that impacts your P & L, let them see where the numbers were, are, and need to be. Performance goals - how did the operation perform in the past, where it is now, and where it has to be in the future. If you don't share this information, goals become meaningless exercises that usually end in failure.

Most importantly, once you've shared the information, get your people involved in the developing their own goals. When they write down their own goals – the ones you've approved and endorsed - they own them. Ownership leads to commitment. Commitment breeds success.

Don't set goals that are impossible to reach. You want as many people to reach their goals as possible – with some stretch, of course. And make sure the goals work to better the employee, the customer, and the success of the operation.

Your job as a manager is to help your people track their progress toward their goals - not as a watchdog or nag, but as a mentor, resource, and coach. Offer friendly reminders and suggestions. Give good examples. Recognize and praise their progress.

It's up to you to see that goals aren't ignored until the next performance appraisal. It's up to you to make goals happen. You share that responsibility equally with each of your employees. If you relinquish your role in reaching your operation's goals, don't expect your people to maintain their enthusiasm for them.

H...HOSPITALITY

It's the name of our business...and don't ever forget it! Your guests come to you for entertainment, for a respite from everyday cares and problems, for comfort in a strange city, for an enjoyable getaway, for a pleasant experience, for a memorable event.

You cannot afford to let your needs, concerns, systems, and rules ever get in the way of their enjoyment and pleasure.

Your goal must be to treat all customers who visit your operation as if you invited them into your own home. They must all receive an individualized greeting, which includes a cheerful welcome and a big smile that comes from both the mouth and the eyes.

If you have invited them into your home, how long do you think you'd make them wait before you opened the door and greeted them? How long do some of your guests wait before someone acknowledges their presence and welcomes them? If they were in your home, you would quickly make them comfortable...hang up their coats, settle them into their guestroom, show them around. And just as quickly, you'd get them a refreshment of their choice. You'd make sure they feel wanted, appreciated, that they were an important visitor.

Ever walk into a typical restaurant two minutes before closing time? How often do you truly feel welcomed?

Part of your home-style hospitality involves determining your guests' likes and dislikes, catering to them in a way that best addresses *their needs and wants.* If you offered a meal, you would be sure that everything was totally to their liking - cooked as they liked it and accompanied only by the best you had to offer.

If they were spending the night, you'd surely check for extra pillows or blankets and offer special, "company-only" toiletries.

You would certainly know what was happening in your community, perhaps even offer a tour of the area. You'd provide insights into events and give directions, if so desired. You'd always do something special - that little extra that says, "you're always welcome here!"

The restaurateur, Hernando Courtright, had a great slogan for his place: *Mi casa es su casa.* My house is your house. That, I submit, in a nutshell, is what this business is all about.

Unfortunately, I don't think enough of us really know what business we are in, day to day.

We cannot afford to let our controls, cash reports, inventories, people problems, equipment failures, rules, or regulations overshadow our efforts to make our guests the total focus of our hospitality. Not now! Not ever!

H...HORSE SENSE

The best education in the world, that MBA from the best business school in the country, or a degree from Europe's finest culinary academy, will not guarantee success in the Hospitality Industry.

No, I'm not discounting the importance of a formal education - including at least four years of college. You'll need those credentials to succeed in any field today. But ours is not a world of theories or indisputable laws of nature that can be learned from books. We deal with constantly changing environments, a nearly endless variety of raw ingredients, and the fragile egos of employees, customers, and bosses.

The successful manager has the common sense - the horse sense, a combination of intelligence (theory) and experience (practice) - to make sure that every decision results in a win-win-win outcome for everybody - employees, customers, supervisors.

Whenever you're faced with a decision, take the few extra seconds needed to ask yourself how this will impact on your employees, and guests. How will they perceive the change? How will they react? Is this really the best decision or just the easiest one for you? What does your gut tell you? Listen to it...it's usually right on target.

But be careful. You can't wait forever to make a decision. The longer we delay, the greater the problem or challenge becomes. Just be sure to use all of your senses in making decisions, including the most important one - *horse sense!*

H...HOT

You serve hot food hot!

You serve cold food cold!

You don't hire warm bodies!

End of discussion.

I...iNCONSiSTENCY

It's a major problem in our industry. Our lack of consistency has given rise to alternative markets – to a burgeoning home meal replacement industry; to highly successful gourmet prepared food departments in supermarkets; to no-frills, inexpensive (read budget) motels and hotels.

On the other hand, exceptional consistency – in price/value, quality, and performance - is why true 5-star operations - at any price (read high **or** low-priced) - always have more business than they can handle.

Customers quickly grow tired of operators they cannot depend on to deliver a consistent product every time they visit. One day, the experience is worth every penny; the next is a total disaster - often at a premium price and an expected tip to boot!

When a guest enjoys your place, he expects it to be just as good the next time...maybe even better. If it doesn't meet his expectations, your credibility is immediately undermined.

Consistency is a management function. Your baby. The buck stops with you. In most cases, it comes down to a simple system of daily expectation and inspection...by YOU! Consistent expectations followed by consistent inspections.

The only change that most customers look forward to is the daily changing list of menu specials. That's a pleasant signal that management respects the customer.

Consistency. We're not talking nuclear science here!

I...iNTEGRiTY

Integrity is vital, no matter what business you're in. When you are dealing in an extremely people- and customer-intensive service industry like ours, it's absolutely critical.

Lie to your customers and they'll find ways to get even – they'll leave you in the blink of an eye. They have plenty of options to replace you. Lie to your employees and you've lost them. Lie on your menu and it can cost you a bundle. Lie to the Liquor Board, and you've lost a license.

In today's litigious society, whenever you do anything wrong – whether your fault or not - and someone is ready to sue. Do you think they'll go after the waiter or cook for that paper clip in the salad when they can sue the owner?

Let's talk about customers first. They trust you. They expect you to deliver exactly what you promise. They expect you to know your purveyors and their products so well that you'll always buy products free from contamination or harmful ingredients. They expect your employees to know how to safely handle your products; how to prevent food-borne illnesses. If they suffer from allergies, they expect your employees to know recipes and ingredients that may trigger negative reactions. Above all, they expect to get good value for dollars spent. Repeat: they trust you. The easiest way to lose customers - by the busload - is to rip them off with unrealized promises and exorbitant prices.

When you say its crab, make sure it is crab, not surimi. When you advertise a half-pound hamburger, it had better be 8 oz. When you write a wine list, don't try to mark it up 3 or 4 times what you paid. If you guarantee satisfaction, don't add lines of tiny print listing all of the exclusions and disclaimers. It's easy - just give them what they want and are paying for - good value.

Your employees are even more sensitive. Want to blow your entire credibility and reduce your operation's morale to somewhere lower than the pits? Start making promises you have no intention of keeping. "Sure, you can have every other Saturday and Sunday off." "Of course, all of our servers make over $100.00 a shift!" "O.K., I'll order that silverware we need first thing in the morning."

You must have a suggestion box, but don't put it up unless you plan to take their suggestions seriously. Don't boast about upcoming changes that never happen. Don't hide your operating results from them because you're afraid they might rip you off. (They can't be effective in helping you solve problems without accurate background information.) Don't concoct glorious bonus programs with goals you know no one can achieve.

Always remember your employees' Golden Rule:

I will do unto my customers as management does unto me.

Trust! Honesty *is* still the best policy. It's one you can never violate or contradict. Whether it's with your employees, your boss, the news media, your customers, your family, or anyone else you run across. Lies, deceit, dishonesty – call it what you will – they all eventually backfire. Nine times out of ten, when it happens, you're the one in the line of fire.

I... iNTERViEWiNG

Lots of us experience exceptionally high turnover rates. Many of us accept it as a fact of doing business. We usually try to blame it on competition, either in or outside, our industry. Don't look for excuses or scapegoats. Doesn't work. The number one cause of turnover? Poor training (see **Turnover**). The second leading cause? Poor, ineffective interviewing. (**Keep reading.**)

A lot of us find ourselves so short of help that we hire the next warm body through the door. You know: Stick a mirror under his nose - if it clouds up, hire him!

Then we wonder what happened when the performance is subpar, or the new employee leaves after a few days. Didn't we find out what the person was really looking for? Didn't we explain to him what our needs were and what we needed him for? Answer: We never took enough time to determine whether the prospective employee was a good bet, a good fit, someone worth training properly.

If you want to seriously reduce your turnover - possibly by up to 30% - if you want to hire the best employees - if you want to create a team that will help your operation grow – then you must be willing to invest significant time and effort into interviewing. No ifs, ands, or buts!

No, it's not easy! Most managers think they need interview only when they need a replacement employee. Sorry, wrong idea! With the crazy turnover levels in this business, you must interview year-round. People are changing jobs all the time – and that includes the best employees – yours and your competition's. The chances are not very good that the employees you want most will be looking for a job at precisely the time you need someone.

Whenever someone walks in your front door looking for work, whether you need her or not, spend a few minutes talking to her, just to find out if she'd be worth talking to. If nothing else, at least get the applicant to fill out an application. Caution: Make sure she fills out that application in your operation. How else can you be sure if the applicant did, in fact, fill out the form herself? It also gives you immediate feedback on reading and writing skills, organization, and even thoroughness.

If the applicant looks like she merits some of your time, schedule an appointment when you can devote some quality time to the interview

- time free of distraction, time when you are in the mood to interview. Plan to spend at least 45 minutes. You want to get to know her through her words and expressions, not just the application. Use her application as a source for interview topics. ("I see on your application that you left your last job after only two months. How come?")

If considering her for a sales position, you want to test self-confidence, conversation skills, and sales ability. For almost any position, you are looking for qualities such as high energy, integrity, team-orientation, and pro-business attitude. You can't validate these traits from a paper application.

Once your interview is complete, check references. As frustrating as this task may be, you will always learn something from a previous employer. Pay special attention to how they answer and how they don't your questions. Former employers almost always have something to say about employees they hated to lose; they almost always hedge about saying anything positive about employees they were happy to lose. By the way, talk to the immediate supervisor, not the human resource office.

Here are a few thoughts on how to conduct a proper interview:

☛ Try to interview at the time the prospective employee will actually be working. After all, if you are looking to hire a breakfast server, don't you want to know what your customers will be seeing at 6:30 in the morning?

☞ Be on time and treat the prospect as you would a customer. This is your first impression too. Make it a good one. You want the prospect to be excited about you and your operation. Make him feel unimportant to you and you become less important to him as well. Interviewing is a two-way street. You're looking for a match that works for both parties.

☞ Provide a private area, free from distractions. Focus only on the prospect.

☞ Make sure the prospect does at most of the talking. Shoot for 80 per cent. It's your job to determine what she has to offer.

☞ Remember, if the candidate does not look, smell, or sound good during the interview, *it won't get any better!* You don't have the time to remake Eliza Doolittles!

☞ Review the Job Description thoroughly during the interview. The prospect must know exactly why you're hiring her and what is expected of her.

☞ Finally, when the interview is over, ask yourself this question: *"Would it "bother me if this individual went to work for one of my competitors?"*

If the answer is "yes," hire him. If the answer is "no," let that person go work for the competition.

J... JOB DESCRIPTION

J.R.D., J.D., Job Card, whatever you call it, the *Job Description* is one of the most important tools you have for making sure that your job - and those of your employees - are done properly.

If your company does not have a J.D. for everyone - write them now.

If they aren't current or haven't been touched in years - revise them now.

If you haven't reviewed yours or those of your employees - review them now.

The Job Description is *the* communication vehicle for effective management of your employees.

Its first use is during the interview. By reviewing the J.D. with the prospective employee, you can give him a detailed understanding of what's expected on the job. By reading through it, you eliminate the surprises that may surface on the first day of work. No more "You didn't tell me that I had to do *that!*"

Next, review the J.D. with the new employee one more time orientation. Your expectations, as set forth in the J.D., become the basis for your training program. The review gives employees yet another reminder of what they need to accomplish in order to become proficient at their jobs. It also establishes the basis for future performance appraisals. If they don't know what they are expected to do, you can't reasonably expect them to do it. Your employee's ability to execute the tasks on the Job Description, combined with his attainment of personal objectives, will affect how you rate him during his performance review and determine his future with your company.

Want to develop the best team you can? The first step is making sure that everyone knows his or her role in the organization. That's what the Job Description is for.

What's the format of a good Job Description? Let's take a stab at it.

⇄ The J.D. should be easy to read and understand. Try to keep it to one page.

⇄ Be as specific as possible. Include a brief paragraph summarizing the job. List the specific tasks to be completed.

☞ Make sure you include the desired end result as well as the process. For example, in addition to the proper way to operate the dishmachine, the dishwasher's J.D. should include a line that states:

"Provides clean, sanitary dishes to assure prompt, safe food service to our guests."

☞ For a server, along with the proper steps of good service, always be sure to include items like:

"Strives to develop long-term positive relationships with your guests."

"Optimizes your sales on every party by learning what they are in the mood for and suggesting menu item which best reflect their desires and needs. Remember expensive is not always better." And "Remember that our goal is 100% guest satisfaction."

☞ Make sure you include job requirements such as: "Must be able to work entire shift on your feet." "Must be able to lift items weighing 25#." "Must be comfortable selling our products to guests."

☞ You may even want to include certain personality traits that fit the particular job; smiles easily, enjoys working with the public, organized, works well under pressure, works well with children, etc.

☞ Pay attention to ADA regulations. Don't include descriptives that violate an individual's rights.

☞ Don't forget, the more specific the J.D., the easier it is to rule out prospects that are not able to perform the tasks spelled out in it.

☞ Include any prerequisites required, such as previous experience, writing skills, education level, proficiency in a language (including English).

☞ Make sure the J.D. includes two signature lines - one for the employee, another for the manager who reviews it with the new hire. Keep a signed copy in the employee file.

If you need help in writing your job descriptions, the NRA has an excellent, inexpensive resource called *Model Position Descriptions for the Foodservice Industry.* It is loaded with sample J.D.'s. Use them as a guide; massage them to fit the specific requirements of your operation.

The bottom line on Job Descriptions ... **You gotta have 'em!"**

K... K.i.S.S.

Keep It Simple and Stupid!

Is this really the true formula for success in the Hospitality Industry?

Think about it:

★ The simpler your menu descriptions, the easier it is for your guests to understand them.

★ The easier it is to do business with you, the more your customers will enjoy doing just that.

★ The simpler your policies and procedures, the faster your employees can learn and master them.

★ The simpler your food recipes, the better the raw product you must use, the better the flavors, and the more appreciative the guests.

★ The simpler your pricing system, the easier for your employees to explain checks to their guests.

★ The fewer your rules and regulations, the easier they are to enforce.

★ The shorter your menu offering, the easier it is to do everything better than your competitors.

★ The more uncluttered your advertising, the easier for guests to understand your message.

★ The easier it is for your guests to check in and out of your hotel, the more they will enjoy their entire stay.

★ The simpler your overall concept, the easier it is to execute.

When you carefully analyze what makes one company or operator more successful, it really comes down to the ability to do all the simple little things just a tiny bit better than everyone else.

If you're in a turnaround situation, try adopting the Japanese formula of *Kaisen* - everyone in the company is strives to do each little task they do just a little bit better every day. Before you know it, you will be the best of the best. Believe it!

L ...LEADERSHIP

The dictionary defines leadership as "the ability to lead." So, what's the big deal? Your employees define leadership differently: it's the example you set for them, day in and day out.

Want your employees to be professional? You have to be professional yourself, *at all times.* How you act and react is how everyone you come into contact with will act and react - fellow managers, your boss, your customers, and most importantly, your employees.

If you want your employees to pay attention to sanitation, you can't walk past that scrap of paper on the floor, fail to notice the smudge on the glass of the front door, or leave a cigarette butt on the sidewalk. Pick up the paper and cigarette butt; wipe off that smudge.

If you want your employees to greet your guests with a big, sincere smile and a warm welcome, you need to do it first. Don't forget to greet your employees that same way when they come in the door every morning!

If you want your food, beverage, payroll, or paper costs to improve, let your employees know that they are critical. Show the same daily concern that you expect from your employees.

If you ever have to freeze wages, don't spend frivolously in any area.

If you want your employees to serve your guests only the best foods and beverages, you must buy only the best, provide excellent recipes, and be there to check on the finished product before it's served to the guest.

If you want your people to be proud of where they work, you must show them that you are proud of them and give them something to be proud of. Set the example. Exhibit your own pride in your people and operation. No complaining, excuses, or gossip!

Trust me, your people take notice of *everything you do.* They follow your lead - for better or worse! How you lead is how they follow.

The unspoken motto is "Do as I do and say!" It's the secret of effective leaders.

M. MANAGING YOUR BOSS

When you're promoted to the position of Manager, it normally takes some time to figure out how you're going to do what you have been told to do: manage the employees who are now reporting to you. (In some cases, these were recently your peers.) There's no question about it; that's exactly what you are being paid to do.

However, if you really want to be effective in your new position, you must learn to manage both up and down the chain of command.

Learning to manage your boss can make your job much easier. It will also make your boss's job easier. It will even make your employees' lives easier and their performances more productive.

How?

Well, when you first become a manager - or start a new management assignment - over-communication is extremely important. It's to your advantage if you initiate most of this over-communication between you and your new boss. If you do not effectively take advantage of this initial orientation period, your chances of long-term success drop precipitously.

Immediately learn your boss's priorities, idiosyncrasies, strengths, and weaknesses. Let your boss know the same information about you. Don't try to convince her that you can walk on water, if you can't. Don't promise quick changes in performance before you have even met the staff. Worst of all, don't try to outdo or upstage the boss. Those kinds of tactics not only will make your life miserable; they may lead to complete failure.

So thoroughly communicate with your boss. Learn how you can complement each other, where your strengths will compensate for her weaknesses and vice versa. Learn what your boss's goals and needs are, then work together to accomplish them.

Most problems within a business come from poor communication. In fact, some experts estimate that employees spend upwards of 40% of their time re-doing things they did wrong the first time because they didn't fully understand the directions. When your boss gives directions, make sure that both of you are on the same wavelength. Ask questions; repeat the directions. It will save you a lot of anguish. This feedback helps you understand what's fully expected of you. It also gives your boss time to reevaluate her direction –

time to modify, refine, confirm, or even discard it.

Keep your boss informed about events or activities occurring on your "watch." Surprises are bad for business (and your reputation), especially when they involve you or your employees. Be professional... not a snitch. Don't cry "Wolf!" Don't panic. Don't waste everybody's time reviewing normal events.

Make sure that you keep in touch on a daily basis regarding exceptional events, progress on key projects, and anything you suspect could impact negatively on either guests or employees. You'll earn your boss's trust and respect for your interest, commitment, and professionalism.

It also helps if you learn to spot the danger signals of an emergency; that's the first step to prevent it from happening.

When you approach your boss with a problem, or a potential problem, always be sure to come equipped with a well-thought-out solution to that problem. By offering your thoughts - a viable action plan that makes sense to you - you'll make your boss's job easier. You'll also eliminate unnecessary conflicts, false starts, and doing things you don't enjoy. Your boss will appreciate it, too!

It's a good idea just to keep your boss abreast of how well your team is doing. You're not bragging; you're giving credit where it's due. By providing her with regular updates, you can effectively eliminate false starts and stops. You keep the whole operation moving in a consistent direction. The last thing you want to do is to implement a new program, only to find out that your boss really wanted something else.

Good, solid, ongoing communication with your boss is the best answer.

You can never communicate too much with her, unless, of course, you are bothering her with all of the minor decisions she thought it was your responsibility to handle.

Share gossip with her? *Big mistake.*

As you continue to develop a trusting relationship with your boss, you'll learn her likes and dislikes. Capitalize on this information. Take over the tasks she doesn't care for. You'll gain her respect. Use this strategy to your advantage, but don't abuse it. You'll find that your career can only benefit from your efforts. The more you take on, the greater the potential rewards.

M...MOMENTS OF TRUTH

The expression, *Moments of Truth,* is credited to the former Chairman of Scandinavian Air Systems, Mr. Jan Carlzon. He coined it to refer to any instance when a customer has an opportunity to draw a conclusion or establish an opinion about your operation, people, management, products, or value. He included features as diverse as advertising, color of product, pricing, uniform style, smiles, and even maintenance or the companies with whom you do business.

In our business, we experience thousands of these moments of truth every day of the week.

Here are a few:

In what media do your ads appear and what do they promise?

How many rings before your phone is answered? Who answers it? What do they say?

How does your parking lot look when guests arrive and depart?

How easy are you to find?

Who greets your guests? How are they greeted? Where are they greeted?

Do you have a large, imposing, intimidating Host desk?

How long does it take for a server to greet guests?

Does your bar have "bar odor?"

Are doors clean and open - both doors on double doors?

Does your drinking water smell fresh and wholesome?

Are menus clean and in good repair?

Are lobby flowers fresh and attractive?

Are prices accurate and fair?

Is a manager present and active in guest areas?

Do guests receive a warm welcome, "Thank you," and an invitation to return?

Is the parking lot fully lighted and safe after dark?

There are several hundred moments of truth involved in every guest visit. It's your job to make sure they are all positive - all the time.

N...NAMETAGS

In my humble opinion, every employee should wear a nametag, including you. The least you should do is make sure that every employee (including you) introduces himself to any new guest he comes in contact with.

A nametag gives the customer a feeling of control and that's exactly where control should be! No more "Hey you!" or snapping of fingers. No more asking, "Can you find my waiter?" No more staff members hiding behind a shield of anonymity.

Now guests can give you more accurate and timely feedback about their experience, be it a complaint or a compliment. Next time they visit, they can ask for their favorite server by name. They can tell others to ask for her as well.

Psychologists tell us that using one's name is the best way to "stroke" an individual. It makes your guest feel important when we use her name. It has the same effect when an employee hears his name and when guests know him by name. Establishing those sorts of relationships between employees and guests results in vast improvements in service. No server, no busser, no bellman or chef is going to ignore the needs of a guest who knows his or her name.

N...NETWORKiNG

I could cover this topic in four little word... "ya gotta do it!"

I've had the pleasure of dining at the best table at one of the most prestigious restaurants in Paris, La Tour d'Argent, because of my network.

I've brought over $250,000.00 in additional business to a restaurant just by networking with a service club.

I've solved personnel, supplier, and equipment problems with the help of my network of friends and associates.

I've secured reservations in hotels and restaurants for important guests when none were available because of my network.

I've observed attendees at my workshops check references, buy ovens, and even find new jobs, just by doing a little networking during breaks.

I've seen managers find the funds they need to open their own operations by networking with their customers.

There's very little that can't be done through an effective network. Yes, it does take some effort, some time, and a lot of sincere, unconditional giving on your part to do it right. But, I've learned that whenever you get involved with a good cause or an activity just for its sake, or give just for the sheer idea of it, your investment always comes back to you ten-fold.

All of your staff members should belong to service organizations in your community. You must belong to and be proactive in the local, state, and national hospitality associations. You must volunteer in local business organizations. Find the time and do it *without expecting a return.* Then, watch what happens!

O...ORIENTATION

Once you have hired your new employees, the key is to keep them and make them productive members of your team. You want to mold them as quickly as possible into contributing members of that team. How do you do that quickly and effectively?

Here's how: A professionally delivered, well-designed orientation.

You say, "Who has the time? They'll pick up what they need from the other employees sooner or later." Right?

Wrong! Bad move! Don't do it! It's a very costly mistake!

Once you've convinced a prospective employee to join your team, you want to be sure that your investment in time, energy, and - yes - money, pays dividends. The easiest way to build up immediate loyalty and interest in achieving success is to make the new employee feel important from day one. That's what orientation is all about.

Who should conduct the orientation?

My first choice is always the owner, if at all possible. That shows the new employee that she is important and not just another number. If not the owner, it should be the most senior manager on the team. Once she's completed the verbal portion of the orientation, she or the new employee's immediate supervisor should conduct a tour of the operation.

What is involved in the orientation? **A lot!**

Here's the opportunity to ensure that your rules and regulations are communicated the way you want them communicated; not translated into "what you can get away with" by tenured employees.

Here's the opportunity to establish the role of the employee on your team and how he interfaces with the rest of the team.

Here's the opportunity to present your Mission Statement and how you view your position in the marketplace.

Here's the opportunity to establish the professionalism of your operation.

Here's your opportunity to convey the message that our industry provides great opportunities for advancement and success, that your employees can have an outstanding and rewarding career, that it's not just a stopping-off place while looking for that first "real" job.

Here's the opportunity to position the employee in a learning mode, to establish a desire to be the best, to become a team player, to settle in for a nice, long productive stay with you.

What do you cover in an orientation?

Here's a partial list. See if you can add more.

Mission Statement
Employee rules and regulations
Wages and how increases are earned
Benefits
Where to park
Sick days and call-in policies
Vacation
Employee meals
Sexual Harassment policies
Pay day policies
Community orientation
Employee phone usage
Facility tour and introduction to fellow
employees
Who reports to whom
Scheduling procedures
Special requests
Future growth potential and how to get
there

Most importantly...a re-review of the Job Description and a discussion of how the employees' job fits into and influences the success of the overall operation.

Is it time-consuming? You bet, but it's worth every minute you put into it. Just try it and see what a difference it makes in your new employees...and even in your old ones, as well!

P ...PERFORMANCE APPRAISAL

When it comes to your job as a manager, nothing is scarier – or causes more stress and anxiety - than those dreaded Performance Appraisals. They're so time consuming. They involve confrontation. They take a long time to prepare for. They involve commitment, compassion, and thoughtful discussion. They require you to follow up on the evaluation (the performance appraisal) and the goals discussed – the ones achieved and the ones missed or neglected.

But...they have got to be done...and hopefully at least twice a year, if not more often.

The benefits far outweigh the pain. They maintain the motivation of your employees. They keep open those all-important lines of communication. They provide a forum for formal recognition of success. They provide learning opportunities – the give and take of ideas and suggestions - for both you and the employee. They help you determine staffing needs. Most importantly, however, they let your employees know how they are doing in your eyes. And when you make sure they involve self-evaluation, they cause the employee to seriously evaluate their own feelings about their performance.

Trust me, performance appraisals are well worth the effort.

So how do you do them well?

➢ Be prepared. Know ahead of time what you plan to discuss and evaluate. Unless you know how your employee has actually performed, your evaluation won't be of much use. Be sure to take all the time you need to really evaluate the employee. Notes jotted down in the employee's file about her behavior – both exemplary and inadequate - during the previous several months help avoid using "last impressions."

I had a boss once who always showed up without having prepared an actual evaluation. He'd look at me and say, "Let's use yours for our discussion." Do you think I took my evaluation seriously? No way!

➢ Allow enough time. Make sure the appraisal is in a private space, with no distractions. You want to assure the employee that this is a meaningful use of your time and his - something to be taken seriously. It also reminds him that he is important to you and the company.

➢ Give the employee plenty of notice and plenty of time to complete the self-evaluation. Be sure you both use the most current job description and personal goals.

➢ Plan your approach to the evaluation. Know ahead of time what your game plan needs to be. Is the employee an all-star? Does the employee have serious performance flaws? Each must be approached differently, with a different end result in mind. Have a pretty good idea of how you plan to end your discussion.

➢ When you start the appraisal, be sure to remind the employee why she's there. This is a review of her performance, her contributions. Remind her of the criteria. You may even want to refresh her on past reviews.

➢ Accentuate the positive. Use positive reinforcement as much as possible. This is a perfect time to let her know the number of times you caught her doing something right.

➢ Don't avoid the negatives, but remember, it's your job to criticize the performance, not the person. This keeps the appraisal on a professional level and prevents it from deteriorating into a finger-pointing session. If there are serious problems, involve the employee in finding solutions. If the situation is so dire you have to fire her, make sure the she fully understands why.

➤ Firing aside, try to end an appraisal session on a positive note by developing a game plan for improvement. That game plan includes how you are going to help. Remember - you are a team member, just like your employee. It's part of your job to try and make everyone successful.

➤ Finally, as you conclude the appraisal, be sure all comments have been properly recorded - in writing. You and the employee sign and date the evaluation. Offer her an opportunity to add her comments, especially if there is disagreement. Remind her that the review will be kept in her personnel file and offer to make a copy for her.

By making the appraisal procedure as professional and meaningful as possible, you will ensure both of you are headed in the same direction; You both understand her performance rating and potential.

Isn't that exactly what you want from your boss?

P ...PERSONAL GROOMING

You know, as I travel the country, I am constantly astonished (and embarrassed) by how employees - and sometimes managers - look in many operations.

I always find it amazing that managers can allow servers or bussers, hostesses or bartenders, desk clerks or bellmen, to face the public looking (and sometimes smelling) like they slept in their uniforms last night.

A wrinkled, soiled shirt or apron, filthy shoes, torn pants, 15 earrings in one ear, etc., is neither attractive nor professional. Most of your guests would agree.

A manager who shows little concern about what his employees look like risks damaging the reputation of his operation. The way your employees look impacts on how your customers rate your overall product and perceive your value. If your dining room employees look lousy, what are your customers to think of the quality of the product coming out of the kitchen?

Your customers want to feel important and special in your place. Let me put it this way: your customers are like your banker. They give you money every day of the week. Would you visit your banker for a loan looking like a slob? Show your banker – your customer – a little respect.

Don't blame slovenly appearance on your employees. They look the way you allow and tell them to look. Employee appearance is totally a management function. Show them how you expect them to look - even before you hire them. Let them know you'll be inspecting constantly.

Keep extra uniforms in the office. Just in case. Keep an iron and ironing board handy and make employees use them, when necessary. You can't supervise appearance from your office. Get out on the floor - front and back – (especially back, if you have a display kitchen) and keep an eye on your reputation. Don't forget, While you've got an eye on your employees, they've also got an eye on you.

 ... QUALITY

Quality is different from value. Value is an ever-changing element, based on your customer's (and employee's) needs, expectations, dollars spent, and impressions of your competition. Quality is an absolute. It's written specifications, recipes, and even Brand Names.

However, the relationship of quality and value and their combined impact determine the success of your operation. If your market is willing to pay your prices for the quality you offer - time and time again - you will be successful. If they don't perceive your quality as being worth your prices, you can't win.

How does your customer judge your quality? It's generally safe to say that most people use tangible - rather than subjective - measures to evaluate your quality:

➲ Do you pour premium liquors?

➲ Do you use prime, or top choice beef?

● Do you use linen napkins?

● Do you use the highest thread count percale sheets?

● Are people well trained to anticipate guests' needs, not just react to them? Are they knowledgeable enough to answer guests' questions? Or at least know who to ask for the answers?

● Do you brew high-quality, fresh, iced tea or use instant?

● Do you use Heinz or just brand-X?

● Do you offer a money-back satisfaction guarantee?

● Do you maintain your facility in top-notch condition at all times?

These are tangible factors, items your guests can see, feel, touch, hear, taste. They can easily compare them to whatever your competition offers.

These same factors allow chains to be as successful as they are. Once your guest finds a quality level where he is comfortable, rest assured he'll return and try their other locations, relatively sure of having a similar experience every time. Whether you like McDonald's or not, you know the hamburger is going to taste the same whether you are in Peoria, Paris, or Palermo.

The value comes into play when the guest determines whether or not that Big Mac is what he wants and can afford.

Your best path to success is to determine what level of quality your target market wants. How do you do that? It's relatively simple - talk to them, watch them, study them. Watch what competitors they use...and how often. Find out where your customers live, what cars they drive, what clothes they and their kids wear, where they work and for whom?

The information you gather will provide you with insights into the level of quality you must offer in order to satisfy the value your customers expect. Remember though, you must really get to know your market. No sense providing a quality that your market cannot afford. Don't provide mediocrity to a market that despises the commonplace.

Today, a lot of markets are made up of the "eternally cash-poor" - people living well beyond their means - trying desperately to keep up with the Jones's. They may have those "Champagne dreams," but are barely able to afford the root beer reality.

Once you know your real guests, do everything you can to stay in sync with their perceptions - and expectations - of quality. Better yet, stay a step ahead; try to embellish the quality, but maintain the value. In other words, try to exceed their expectations every time they come in to your place.

R...RECIPE

I know a lot of chefs and bartenders who hate that word! "It limits my creativity!" My guests want it differently!" "My version is better!"

If these are valid comments, it's your job to do something about it! But the answer is not to give up recipes. The answer is to modify the standards to suit the need.

If the chef's recipe is better than yours, change your recipe. If most of your guests don't like the way you mix your Martinis, change your recipe to reflect their preference.

Guests demand excellent, CONSISTENT products priced fairly. Guests don't like surprises. They want to know that the Pasta Primavera will taste the same every time they order it. That they will pay the same price for the same item each time they order it.

They want to know that the Pina Colada will taste the same, no matter which bartender makes it. They want to know that the service will be at the same level of excellence, no matter when they are there or who's with them.

Consistency continues to challenge all of us. Lack of it drives guests away from our doors and into supermarket gourmet counters for food to go. It drives them from high-priced luxury hotels to mid-price no-frills properties. If you don't deliver consistency, don't expect guests to pay your premium rates or tip your employees. That goes for every level of service, whether you're fast food or the most luxurious hotel in the country.

The answer really isn't that difficult. Hire the best employees. Train them better than anyone else. Arm them with high standards of performance - RECIPES!

Recipes for all food products.

Recipes for all beverage products.

Recipes for proper service of those products.

Recipes for treating guests with the best possible hospitality.

Recipes for getting promoted within your company.

Recipes: they're the standards you establish, repeat and repeat and repeat, and live by.

Studies have shown, over and over, that the higher your standards, the better your product. An excellent product is one that you can rely on time after time, whether it's a car, a toaster, a restaurant, or a hotel! However, if you don't lay out the recipes for your employees, even the best raw products can be improperly prepared or utilized.

Here are some final thoughts on recipes. Write them down. Written recipes help you assure consistency in communicating what you're all about. They give everybody the same resource. They eliminate the response, "But you told me to do it that way."

One caution, however... I don't know how many times owners have told me that their executive chef, or their partner, or a trusted employee, left the operation with the only copies of the signature recipes. Don't let that happen to you.

Trust me. You want to be great. Write a recipe for it!

(see **Standards**)

S...STANDARDS

You've got to have them! And you don't have them until they are written down!

Minimum standards include...

* Food & Beverage recipes. Yes, even for the bar drinks!

* Service timing. Give the customer control of timing!

* Hospitality. That includes the reason for a big smile and a cheerful greeting.

* Appearance. Be thorough. Don't forget the daily bath and the earrings.

* Integrity. Stress both the rationale for it and consequences for abuse!

* Selling Efforts. Suggestive selling is not a turn-off when done correctly. Servers need to know they are judged on sales efforts and results.

❖ Teamwork. I don't know of any other way to be successful!

❖ Attendance. Being there and being there on time. Frequent tardiness impacts on morale.

❖ Temperature. Hot food hot. Cold food cold.

❖ Safety... of food, property, and people

❖ Sanitation. It's everybody's job.

OOPS! I almost forgot! Back to the beginning of this chapter. You don't have standards until you communicate them to all of your employees, until you establish your performance expectations fully, and until you inspect for them every day.

S...SUGGESTION BOX

Whoa, you're mistaken! You won't just get cards from wise guys and little old ladies who have nothing better to do than tell you how to run your business. That'll never happen if you treat your suggestion box program professionally and reward worthwhile suggestions!

There are two groups of "experts" who know the problems and opportunities in your everyday business as well as, if not better than, you do - your customers and your front-line employees.

Once you tap into these phenomenal resources, the sky's the limit! If you're afraid to ask for suggestions face-to-face (and a lot of us are because we assume we won't get candid responses), at least place a box in both the guest area and near the employee time clock.

Personally hand out comment cards and pencils. Include only one or two questions and leave plenty of room for comments.

How about questions like... "What could we have done to make your experience today even better?" or "How can we make your job easier?"

Fringe benefit: If you ask your guests to sign their comment card and provide a mailing address, you're on your way to building a data base of customers you can target with future promotions.

Then comes the real challenge: Responding to the answers and suggestions. Acknowledge, but don't overwork the ones that aren't relevant or are misdirected. Heed the ones that are sincere, show genuine concern, and surface more than once. You must sincerely want to improve your operation...and be willing to share the credit and rewards of your suggestive program with those who contribute.

One point to remember: you'll always get more response from those folks at the extremes – the extremely happy and the extremely ticked-off. Look for common threads. Do some additional research on the heavy-duty complaints. Make that extra effort to contact the guest to see if you're getting the entire story.

Employees? Some sort of bonus. Customers? A thank you for the thought, or an apology (including your remedy) for a complaint.

T ...TURNOVER

It's our industry's biggest headache. Studies report turnover of anywhere from 100% to 300% annually. Many of us just write it off as just a part of working in the Hospitality business.

Well, it just doesn't have to be that high. There are plenty of great examples of operators with five to 10 percent turnover, even less! And you can be there as well.

Let's take a closer look at TURNOVER.

TRAINING:

The number one cause of turnover is *job ambiguity!* If an employee isn't trained well enough to reach a comfort zone in his job, the tendency is to go somewhere else to find that zone. You want him moving up to your *all-star zone!* To do that, you must train constantly. Right! That means forever!

UNDERSTANDING:

Understand your employees are individuals, not robots called upon to execute commands.

Understand that they each learn at a different rate.

Understand that they each have different hot buttons.

Understand that they are motivated by different rewards and needs.

Understand that they have different goals.

Understand that each has a different personality and background.

Understand that they each hear what you say differently.

REWARDS & RECOGNITION:

The best reward you can give your employees is recognition (publicly, of course) when they do their jobs well or go beyond the call of duty. That pat on the back goes farther than anything else you can do for them ... providing, of course, that you are already paying them fairly.

No surprises:

Your employees need to know that they can depend on you to react the same way every time a specific situation arises. Good or bad, they know how you will or will not respond. Inconsistency dilutes trust and drives good employees right out the door.

Openness:

You can never be *too* open or *too* honest with your employees. They can't help you solve your problems and challenges if you don't "clue them in." Once you create that feeling of trust among your employees, they'll be with you forever. The only way to create that commitment is through openness.

Vitality:

In this business, you lead by example. Show your excitement. Reveal your enthusiasm. Broadcast your energy. Make work fun. This is contagious stuff, powerful motivators - *but only from the top down!* When employees enjoy their jobs and feel a vital part of the organization, they stay in their jobs.

Empower them:

Good employees want to feel important - a vital part of the team. They want to know that you trust them and can't possibly run the operation without them. Empowering them to make decisions is a great way to breed that feeling of importance. But remember, empowerment can happen *only with exceptional training.*

RESPECT:

You've got to earn it from your employees, but you have to give it to them from day one. They want you to treat them like adults, individuals, contributors, and important human beings.

U ... UNIQUE SELLING PROPOSITION

Every operation needs one. What is it? It's something that will keep you in business for a long time. The unique selling proposition is made up of those facets of your business that make you different from all of your competitors. There are so many possibilities that it would take an entire book just to list them. Here are a few just to get you thinking:

- ❑ The best service in the area

- ❑ A spectacular beverage menu

- ❑ A truly unique and outstanding signature menu item

- ❑ A one-of-a-kind view

- ❑ An extremely interesting decor

- ❑ An exceptional value

- ❑ The widest variety of food offerings in your area

- ☐ Unique entertainment

- ☐ The only steakhouse in town

- ☐ The only operation to fly in seafood daily

- ☐ The largest selection of single-malt Scotch in the state

- ☐ A truly unique birthday celebration club

- ☐ Brewing a bunch of beers on premise

- ☐ All you care to eat something or other

- ☐ Free appetizers with a meal

- ☐ The best interactive sports bar in town

- ☐ A hotel room reservations system which "remembers" past guests' specific needs

- ☐ Your turn: _____

Why is it essential to have this unique positioning? COMPETITION! You can either be an also-ran with the rest of the uncreative world, or you can be a leader in the hospitality industry. Do you think, for one moment, that Wolfgang Puck became what he is today by copying what his competitors were doing?

If a certain type of operation does not exist in your marketplace, fill that void, making sure, beforehand, that there's a demand for it. If there are several operations like yours in town, make sure yours is better than all the rest.

The first step: make sure your product is solid - your food is excellent; your drinks taste great; your service is outstanding. You can't accomplish any of these without investments in training (see **Development**) and standards (see **Recipe**). Without both of these, there is no uniqueness. Greatness doesn't just happen. You plan it. You practice it over and over again.

Once you've mastered the basics, compare your operation with that of your competition. Where are you better? Where do you need help? Where are you similar? What makes you different? The factors that make you different are positives, capitalize on them. Make them stronger and even more different.

Want to find out what your points of differentiation are? Ask your employees and guests what makes you different. What makes them come back? What do they like most, least? What needs to be improved? Why do your employees like to work here?

Customers and employees are your best resources. Your customers know your competition; your employees may even have friends who work for them. They know who serves what and who doesn't. Who offers this benefit and who offers that. And so on. Best of all, this information is free – it's literally there just for the asking. No Charge! Downside? Well. There is that occasional blow to the ego when we hear something we didn't want to hear.

Once you have learned about yourself, start improving on your mousetrap. The happier you keep your existing players, both customers and employees, the more they'll generate business for you, both in return business and in recommendations to friend, neighbors, and business associates. And, guess what. The "Unique Selling Proposition" makes it that much easier for them to tell others about you. It gives them something they remember time and time again when they are thinking about going out for dinner or when traveling to your city. They can easily recommend you, just by saying, "You've got to go there, they have the best _____ in town!"

V...VENDORS

Vendors, suppliers, purveyors - whatever you call them, you can't do business without them. They're critical. Whether you succeed or fails is due, in some measure to the relationships you build and nurture with them.

Today, the hot concept is "partnering," working closely with selected vendors to achieve greater sales and profits on both sides of the invoice. The concept is great and it works, as long as you remember that all vendors - just like you - must make a profit.

My recommendation? Limit the total number of vendors you use. One primary vendor in each category, plus one or two secondary (back-up) vendors is probably more than enough. You don't develop vendor loyalty by shopping around only for price. The Chef who shops 12 fish mongers every day and buys on the cheapest price is getting just that - the cheapest fish - not the freshest or the best quality - just the cheapest. And just wait until he's in a bind. Which of those 12 purveyors is going to go out of his way to help him?

Don't forget it costs a vendor plenty of money every time he puts a truck and driver on the road. If you keep requesting deliveries of one or two items, sooner or later, they'll have to find a way to cover their costs. Impose a minimum? Possibly, or just refuse your orders.

On the other hand, don't ever give all of your business to one vendor and just forget about the others. A little competition and an alert buyer are always good for both prices and quality. Check prices with your secondary vendors and let your primary know when he's getting out of line. (By the way, make sure both vendors have a copy of your current purchasing specs. That's essential.) Make sure you also advise vendors of any slippage in quality or service. Be honest. Don't cry wolf just to get attention. You really do want a successful partnership, one that works to everyone's benefit.

Don't be afraid to challenge your vendors to bring you new products, new recipes, or new promotional ideas that will help you build or attract new sales. You'll be amazed at their resources. Also ask them for assistance in employee training. They often have great experts right on staff.

They want to keep your business as much as you want to do business with them. If you develop a relationship on mutual respect, they'll do whatever it takes to service you.

Remember, it's your job to manage your vendors just like you manage your employees. Your goals and their goals need to be the same – sustaining and maintaining the growth of your company.

 ...WINNING RESPECT

Just because you are the manager, doesn't mean everyone respects you. The level of respect you earn is based on how you act every day of the year; the decisions you make; the manner in which you treat your employees, customers, and co-managers. Oops, almost forgot – even your vendors.

Think about it.

W...WORD OF MOUTH

Everyone knows that word of mouth is the best advertising. It is, provided it's *positive word of mouth.*

Bottom line: What people say about you is only as good as their most recent experience with you.

No one succeeds by resting on his or her past reputation. Tony Athanas, owner of the world famous Anthony's Pier 4 in Boston, said it best. As he looked at walls filled with plaques and awards from every foodservice and community association in and around Boston and beyond, he commented: "Those awards don't mean anything - you're only as good as your last meal."

W...WORKING CONDITIONS

Your employees want to work in a clean, organized, safe, secure, pleasant environment - one that positively affects them emotionally, physically and psychologically. As a manager, you provide that environment. If it's not there, they leave. It's as simple as that.

X...."XCEEDING XPECTATIONS"

Did you know that 85 percent of your current guests will eventually leave you if your reputation is just good? That's good - not average or poor! Scary isn't it?

Customer Satisfaction levels are tied to customer expectations:

$$\text{Customer Satisfaction} = \frac{\text{Actual Experience}}{\text{Expectations}}$$

If experience is less than expectations, you have disappointed guests. They might give you one more chance, but after that, forget it... unless the second experience is absolutely sensational.

If the experience is equal to expectations, the customer is merely satisfied. It was good, but not great - not memorable. Ho-Hum! Take it or leave it. Customers just don't remember you when you just meet their expectations.

But, if the experience far exceeds the expectations, people remember you and come back again. Why? Because exceptional experiences are so rare today... and even rarer still when they occur consistently at the same place. It's just too good to be true!

Once you've "knocked their socks off," two or three times, you're on the way to building a loyal customer. They still wonder a little about how long this can last, but the excitement continues to build. They'll even overlook a few minor flaws now and then - or even one total disaster - as long as you are good at your recovery.

Now for the real key! Loyal, regular guests do not remain either loyal or regular unless you recognize and reward their loyalty. Use their names often. Thank them for their patronage. Remember who their favorite server is, what their favorite menu item is, what they like to drink. Ask about family. Ask about business. Remember their special occasions in special ways. Treat them like royalty. They will reward you handsomely in return.

Y...*"YES IS THE ANSWER"*

"Yes is the answer. Now, what is the question?" That has been the operating philosophy of noted restaurateur Michael Hurst for years...and it works.

Our business requires – no, make that demands - a can-do attitude, a desire to make it right, to make it special, to make it positively memorable.

Flexibility is key to satisfying guests today. Remember the old Burger King slogan, "Have it your way?" It's truer today than ever before. Your customers want it their way - what they want, when they want it, and how they want it.

Still got this reminder on your menu - *No substitutions?* Forget about it. How about this one: *Desserts may not be shared?* Gone. Delete it. Customers just don't tolerate silly imperatives any more. There are just too many other operations out there for them to patronize.

Today, you garner undying customer loyalty only when you respond effectively to each customer's needs and wants *when they need them and when they want them.*

Come on now, aren't you the same way?

Z...ZONE

The *ZONE* - it's where you want your people to perform every time they do their jobs.

You've undoubtedly heard how Michael Jordan and other sports superstars brag about "being in the zone" when and where everything clicked perfectly. Well, it's your job to help your employees find and play in a similar zone. There's only one way to get there and that's through outstanding and continuous training. Most importantly, that training must include interactive, participative, kinesthetic learning - R-O-L-E P-L-A-Y.

When was the last time you saw sports teams sitting around reading manuals or watching training tapes between games? Most of the time they're out on the field or court practicing, doing, over and over again.

They practice routine drills. They practice the two-minute drill, a full-court press. They practice handling any situation they might confront during a game. Why? So they can take it in stride if and when it happens. It's no longer a crisis that blows the whole program. It's just a variation on one of the routines they have already practiced.

When you can handle the little things routinely, the big ones look a lot smaller and your guests don't feel the bumps at all.

ABOUT THE AUTHOR

Howard Cutson, FMP, is Principal of Cutson Associates, a customer satisfaction-oriented consulting firm serving the Hospitality Industry. He has spent over 30 years working in all aspects of this industry. He is a former Vice President of Stouffer Restaurants and faculty member at the University of Akron, teaching Hospitality Management and Beverage Management courses.

He is the author of the **Hospitality Role-Play Trainers®**, a unique program designed to improve daily waitstaff training and co-author of **50 Proven Ways to Build Restaurant Sales and Profits, 50 Proven Ways to Build More Profitable Menus, and 50 Proven Ways to Enhance Guest Service.**

Howard lives in Hudson, Ohio with his wife Sharon.

WORKSHOPS...

Howard Cutson is a nationally known speaker and workshop facilitator. He offers programs such as the following:

Full-day Workshops:

People Management 101
Building Your Own All-Star Team
Managing Today's Bar
The Dining Room Server's Refresher Course

Half-day Workshops:

Building Employee Loyalty
Growing Lifetime Customers
Effective Bar Cost Controls
Building Your Bar Sales

One/Two-Hour Presentations:

The Keys to Stronger Relationship Selling
Building Employee Loyalty
Professional Bar Controls
Professional Telephone Skills
Upgrading Your Service Skills
No-Pressure Selling
Building An All-Star Sales Team
Building Bar Sales

Call (800) 776-7988 for more information.

ORDER FORM

Do you need extra copies of this book or any of the Hospitality Masters Press Books?

1-19 copies: $14.95 each
20 or more copies: call
for discounts.
S/H: add $3.00 for single books, $6.00 for multiples.

No.   Book:

___   **The ABC's of Hospitality Management**
___   **50 Proven Ways to Build Restaurant**
        Sales & Profits
___   **50 Proven Ways to Build More**
        Profitable Menus
___   **50 Proven Ways to Enhance Guest**
        Service

Total Order: $ _____
(Ohio residents include 5.75% Sales Tax)

Name:_____

Company:_____

Address:_____

City:_____State:___Zip:_____

Phone:_____Fax:_____

Payment By: Check___ AMEX___ VISA___ MC___

Account No:_____

Exp: _____ Signature: _____

Send or FAX your order to:
Howard Cutson
589 Atterbury Blvd.
Hudson, Ohio 44236-1643
Phone: (800) 776-7988 FAX: (330) 656-3335